The Dad Jokes Book!

800 Dad Jokes for Unceasing Snickers, Smiles, and Sighs of "Not Again!"

Cover design by Aaron Wilkins

Edited by Terrence Bradford

Table of Contents

Prepare to Become the Funniest Person in Any Situation

If one were to embark on a noble quest, diving into the annals of history searching for a universal constant, they might overlook the Pythagoras theorem or the works of Shakespeare, and instead, stumble upon the enduring (and endearingly terrible) dad joke.

Yes, that delightful (or dreadful, depending on your humor threshold) brand of humor that's been passed down through generations, much like a treasured family heirloom or that peculiar gravy boat no one ever uses.

Now, some enlightened individuals might proclaim, "Ah, but not all heroes wear capes; some just arm themselves with dad jokes at family gatherings!" A truer statement has rarely been uttered.

Why, just last week, as I was tightening the screws of a wobbly chair, a nephew remarked, "That chair's just like Grandpa, always on its last leg." And the room burst into laughter, the chair momentarily forgotten.

You see, "Dad Jokes 2024" isn't just a collection of jokes; it's a curated mosaic of memories. The jokes nestled in these pages are akin to those little bubbles of joy we all remember from childhood, or even from last Tuesday. The ones that made milk shoot from our nostrils, or caused a room full of stone-faced board members to erupt in unison.

Young ones, with their budding sense of wit, will find a treasure trove of jokes to share on the playground, ensuring their legacy as the funniest kid in the sandbox. And for the adults? Oh, you're in for a treat.

These jokes will arm you with an arsenal of humor for dinner parties, business meetings, and even those dreaded PTA gatherings. You might even find your teenager admitting, albeit grudgingly, "Okay, that was a good one."

Prepare yourself, dear reader, as you're about to embark on a journey—a riotous expedition where puns reign supreme, and a groan is just as prized as a chuckle.

Grab your favorite armchair, maybe a cup of tea (or something stronger, depending on your day), and let's plunge into a year brimming with merriment!

The Smart Aleck: Wisecracks

One Liners!

Have hope for the future, but maybe build a bomb shelter anyway.

You take away the looks, money, intelligence, charm and success and, really, there's no real difference between me and George Clooney.

I hate when I am about to hug someone really sexy and my face hits the mirror.

It was only when I bought a motorbike that I found out that adrenaline is brown.

A miracle drug is one that has now the same price as last year.

Haircuts are great because I did none of the work, but get all the credit.

I just stare at my desk, but it looks like I'm working.

I used to play tennis, baseball, basketball and chess, but I stopped after my son broke my PlayStation.

When my boss asked me why I showed up late for our Zoom meeting, I told him that he wouldn't believe the network traffic.

Football is a game when 22 big, strong players run around like crazy for two hours while 50,000 people who really need the exercise sit in the stands and watch them.

The greatest miracle in the Bible is when Joshua told his son to stand still and he obeyed him.

The only love triangle I want is a slice of pizza.

Our computers went down at work today, so I had to play Solitaire with a real deck of cards.

I know a lot of jokes in sign language and I guarantee you that no one has ever heard them.

My teacher always tells me to follow my dreams, but she won't let me sleep in class.

A recent study has found that women who carry a little extra weight live longer than the men who mention it.

Living on Earth might be expensive, but at least you get a free trip around the Sun every year.

Statistics show that those who have the most birthdays live the longest!

When my boss asked me who was stupid, me or him, I told him he doesn't hire stupid people.

I play all the right notes, but not necessarily in the right order.

What's a cow's favorite animal?

MOOSE!

I walked past a homeless guy with a sign that read, "One day, this could be you."

I put my money back in my pocket, just in case he's right.

There are three kinds of jobs:

those you shower before, those you shower after... and working from home.

I can totally keep secrets.

It's the people I tell them to that can't.

My wife just found out I replaced our bed with a trampoline.

She hit the roof.

Success is like a fart.

It only bothers people when it's not their own.

Alcohol is a perfect solvent.

It dissolves marriages, families and careers.

If you drink too much alcohol you are an alcoholic.

If you drink too much Fanta, does that make you Fantastic?

You think you love autumn?

My blood type is Pumpkin spice!

It's cleaning day today.

I've already polished off a whole chocolate bar.

I love vegan food!

It makes an excellent side dish to any meat.

My therapist told me the way to achieve true inner peace is to finish what I start.

So far today, I have finished two bags of chips and a chocolate cake.

I feel better already.

Warning!

Birthday donuts will make your clothes shrink!

You need to understand the difference between want and need.

Like I want abs, but I need donuts.

The optimist sees the whole donut.

The pessimist sees the donut hole.

You can look at the solar eclipse directly.

Once with your left eye, once with your right eye.

I've finally saved up enough for solar panels.

Now I just have to afford a house.

Madonna is 54 and her boyfriend's 25.

Jennifer Lopez is 43 and her boyfriend's 26.

So if you're single it's ok, maybe he's just not born yet.

My boyfriend said he wanted more space.

So I locked him outside.

I want to be the reason who makes you look down at your phone and smile...

And then walk into a pole…

Today, my son asked "Can I have a book mark?" and I burst into tears.

11 years old and he still doesn't know my name is Brian.

I love Valentine's Day: the bottle of wine, the heart-shaped ice cream cake...

Taking them home and eating them alone while crying and watching YouTube videos.

Good times.

Got an ice cream for my girlfriend.

Best trade I ever made.

My sister said I'm being immature.

I guess she isn't getting her nose back.

When I was a boy, I had a disease that required me to eat dirt three times a day in order to survive...

It's a good thing my older brother told me about it.

My sinus infection is really getting into the Christmas Spirit.

It's all coming out green and red.

I don't like people who do not cover their mouths and noses when they sneeze.

These people make me sick.

My wife and kids are leaving me because of my obsession with horse racing.

Annnnd…they're off!

"You know, I think it's your turn to pick wild mushrooms." My girlfriend said.

So I gather.

I love being a grandparent in retirement.

I give my grandkids a lot of sugar and then leave them with their parents to deal with them.

Good Morning, workmate!

Being around you has inspired me... to find a job in another state!

I always wanted a life like a Disney princess.

I should have specified not the part where they are stuck at home, cleaning the whole day.

Love is a very complex matter of chemistry.

And that is why my partner treats me like toxic waste!

Love is like farting.

If you have to force it, it's going to end in a mess.

Love is a lot like peeing your pants.

Only you can feel the warm sensation from such an experience.

My kids won't eat their tacos for dinner, so I had to throw them out.

Then I ate their tacos.

Today I made a big pot of pasta,

but when I went to dump the pot into the sink, I think I strained something.

I always seem to say the wrong thing. For example yesterday I complimented my best friend's mustache.

Now she's not talking to me.

The worst part about being a giraffe...

Is having a lot of time to think about your mistakes when you're sinking into quicksand.

I like to wrap myself in a blanket when I work from home.

You could say I now work undercover.

Santa saw your Facebook pictures...

You're getting clothes and a Bible for Christmas.

I burned 2000 calories today.

I fell asleep while baking pizza in the oven.

If you ever feel like your job has no purpose, always remember:

Right now there is someone who is installing a turn signal in a BMW.

They say that two things in life are unavoidable: death and taxes.

At least death only happens once!

Intaxifcation: The wonderful feeling you get when you receive a tax refund until you realize it was your own money in the first place.

Someone once told me that taking money out of your savings account is stealing from your future self.

Well luckily for me my future self won't be able to afford a lawyer to press charges against me.

Can anyone recommend a good bank account?

Mine's run out of money...

Whenever I see a man with a beard, mustache and glasses, I think

"There's a man who has taken every precaution to avoid people doodling on photographs of him."

Last night, I changed a light bulb, crossed a road, walked into a bar and chatted with an Englishman, a Scotsman and an Irishman.

That's when I realized my entire life is a joke...

Dear Students,

I know when you are texting in class. No one just looks down at their crotch and smiles.

Never fight a math teacher.

You'll always be outnumbered.

Dear Math,

I am sick and tired of finding your "x". Just accept the fact that she's gone. Move on dude.

I won a wet t-shirt competition. Guess what I got?

Pneumonia!

My wife told me that women were better at multitasking than men.

So, I told her to sit down and shut up. Guess what?

She couldn't do either.

Diet day 1:

I removed all the fattening food from my house.

It was delicious.

If you ever get cold, just stand in the corner of a room for a while.

They're normally around 90 degrees.

It is generally believed that talking with your mouth full is rude.

Personally, I find talking with your head empty much worse.

If God really made everything…

He's Chinese, right?

Not to brag, but I defeated our local chess champion in less than five moves.

My karate lessons are paying off.

We really should look into colonizing Mars and other planets or moons.

If you look at the studies, 100% of deaths occur here on earth.

I used to be a boy trapped in a woman's body.

But after 9 long months, I was finally born!

The Merry Meateater: Steak Your Claim

One Liners!

If we aren't supposed to eat animals, why are they made of meat?

Your mom's so vegan and fat, she ate a meal and got arrested for deforestation.

What did the vegan say?

I made a big missed steak.

Vegan: People who sell meat are gross!

Non Vegetarian: People who sell fruits and vegetables are grocer.

Why is Veganism like Communism?

They are both fine, unless you like food.

What's the difference between a vegan and a computer programmer?

One is disgusted by a rack of lamb and the other is disgusted by a lack of RAM.

Knock, knock.

(Who's there?)
Lettuce.
(Lettuce who?)
Lettuce eat veggies, I'm vegan!

What's the toughest part of being a vegan?

Apparently keeping it to yourself.

Why do vegans lose their eyesight earlier than meat-eaters?

From reading all those tiny ingredient labels.

How many vegans does it take to eat a bacon cheeseburger?

One if nobody's looking.

What do you call the argument between two vegans?

A plant-based beef.

What's the hardest part about being a vegan?

It is getting up at 4.30am to milk the almonds.

Did you hear about that vegan who was condemning some random guy for drinking milk?

How dairy!

What's the only thing a vegan kills?

A conversation.

Why is almond milk called "almond milk"?

Because nobody could call it "nut juice" and keep a straight face.

Did you hear about the man whose girlfriend really changed after she became a vegan?

It's like he has never seen herbivore.

Why do vegans often look miserable in photos?

They don't like to say 'cheese'.

Why did the cannibal only eat people in comas?

He was going Vegan.

How do you know aliens are not vegan?

Because they haven't contacted us to say it.

What is the most effective way to quit being vegan?

Cold turkey.

Did you hear that vegans will be the first to invent intergalactic travel?

Imagine living in the Milky Way.

Why do people make such a big deal about vegans?

Don't get it, never had a beef with one.

Have you met Bruce Lee's vegan brother?

He's called Broco Lee.

Why are vegan pick-up lines of higher quality than non-vegan pick-up lines?

Because they can't be cheesy!

What's the first rule of the Vegan club?

You tell everyone about the Vegan club.

What do gun owners and vegans have in common?

They're both in your face about how they're not murderers.

A non-vegetarian was asked If he were to be stranded on an island with anyone whom would he prefer.

"A vegan," he said. "Mostly because it's healthier to eat grass-fed meat."

A policeman arrives at the crime scene.

"Now, Madam, can you describe the man who stole your handbag?"

"Oh, it all happened so fast! He pushed me over from behind, I didn't see him at all. One thing though; he was a vegan."

"How do you know that?"

"He told me as he was running off."

What's a vegan's favorite animal?

A high horse.

What does a vegan say after meeting someone new?

"Nice to meat — ew!"

What do you call a vegan burger?

A misteak.

What do you call a vegan-friendly jacket?

A Peta Parka.

An airline employee makes the final boarding call for a flight.

After she finished the announcement, she spots a man running down the concourse towards the gate.

He runs through the boarding area, hurdles a row of empty chairs, and stops at the podium, almost out of breath.

"You just made it!" she says. "Do you have your boarding pass?"

"Oh, this isn't my flight," the man says. "I just wanted to tell you that I'm vegan."

What do you call a vegan lion?

Dead.

What do rappers and vegans have in common?

Fake beef.

What do you call a vegan with diarrhea?

A Salad Shooter.

How do you upset a vegan by email?

Send them some spam.

What did the Vegan DJ say to the crowd?

"Lettuce turnip the beet!"

What do you call an on and off vegan?

Vegemight.

A man went to his doctor.

After several tests, the doctor returned to the exam room and told him "I'm terribly sorry sir but according to our tests you have barely a year left to live."

"That's horrible!" said the man. "Is there nothing I can do?!"

The doctor replied, "Well, my advice is to become a vegan, marry an economist, and move to Iowa."
"Will that cure me?" asked the man

"No," said the doctor "but it'll make that year feel a LOT longer!"

What do you call a vegan dinosaur?

Falafel Raptor.

Why do vegans insist on telling you they are vegan?

They can't bite their tongues.

Did you know that vegans don't live longer?

It just feels like they do.

Two vegans bump into each other at a BBQ.

"We must stop meating like this."

What was Aladdin called after he went Vegan?

Saladdin.

What do vegans get instead of bird flu?

Toflu.

What do you call a vegan chicken strip?

A chicken pretender.

What's the hardest part of making a vegan pizza?

Skinning the vegan.

Did you hear about the serial killer who kidnapped a couple of vegans in his basement?

At least he thinks they're vegan. They keep shouting, "lettuce leaf!"

Did you hear about the vegan transgender?

He was a herbefore.

What does a vegan molester eat?

Gropefruit.

What's the difference between vegans and strippers?

Vegans rub it in your face for free.

What is the most ironic name for a vegan?

Hunter.

Paycheck Playfulness

One Liners!

Maybe if we all sit extremely still, Monday won't be able to see us.

If you think your job sucks, remember whenever a famous personality dies, someone at Wikipedia has to change all the verbs to past tense.

My job is incredibly secure, nobody wants it!

The closest people come to perfection is on an employment application.

When funny Dad came to the bottom of the job application where it says, "Sign Here," he wrote "Scorpio."

When the CEO dropped a brownie on his calculator, he was accused of fudging the numbers.

Claustrophobic people are more productive thinking out of the box.

My boss says I intimidate the other employees, so I just stared at him until he apologized.

I used to work at a fire hydrant factory and couldn't park anywhere near the place.

I work to buy a car to go to work.

I think that if I died and went straight to hell it would take me at least a week to realize I wasn't at work anymore.

My resumé is just a list of things I hope you never ask me to do.

All I'm saying is why blame it on being lazy when you can blame it on being old?

I'm here for whatever you need me to do from the couch.

Sure boss, I'd love to take on some extra work, I have like 7-8 free hours a night where all I do is sleep anyway.

I start every conversation with my employees by saying, "I shouldn't be telling you this" just so I know they will listen.

My doctor told me I needed to break a sweat once a day so I told him I'd start lying to my wife.

If some people didn't tell you, you'd never know they'd been away on vacation.

Yesterday I did nothing and today I'm finishing what I did yesterday.

Nothing ruins a Friday more than an understanding that today is Tuesday.

Laugh at your problems, everybody else does.

He who smiles in a crisis has found someone to blame.

The proper way to use a stress ball is to throw it at the last person to upset you.

If at first you don't succeed, redefine success.

To err is human, to blame it on someone else shows management potential.

A man can do more than he thinks he can, but he usually does less than he thinks he does.

How long have I been working for this company?

Ever since they threatened to fire me.

My boss told me to have a good day.

So I went home.

Boss: "You're fired."

Me slamming a fist on the couch: "You woke me up for this?"

I use artificial sweetener at work.

I add it to everything I say to my boss.

Definition of Boss:

Someone who is early when you are late and late when you are early.

I applied for a job today and they asked for three references.

I wrote, "a dictionary, a Thesaurus, and a map."

There is a new trend in our office; everyone is putting names on their food.

I saw it today, while I was eating a sandwich named Kevin.

If every day is a gift, I'd like a receipt for Monday.

I want to exchange it for another Friday.

Don't be irreplaceable -

if you cannot be replaced, you cannot be promoted.

Some cause happiness wherever they go.

Others whenever they go.

The human brain is a wonderful thing.

It starts working the moment you are born, and never stops until you stand up to speak in public.

I had a job selling security alarms door to door and I was really good at it.

If no one was home I would just leave a brochure on the kitchen table.

Me: "You said dress for the job you want."

Boss: "Give me my clothes back."

At this point in my life, my resume's "special skills" section just says:

"pronounces Massachusetts towns" and "can nap on planes."

I don't understand why people don't like lazy people.

They didn't do anything.

Boss: How can we keep the office clean?

Me: By staying at home.

Me (at work): "I think I'm having a heart attack."

My boss: "Do that on your own time!"

My memory has gotten so bad it has actually caused me to lose my job.

I'm still employed. I just can't remember where.

There was a safety meeting at work today.

They asked me, "what steps would you take in the event of a fire?"

"Big Ones" was the wrong answer.

I once worked as a salesman and was very independent;

I took orders from no one.

How do construction workers party?

They raise the roof.

At my job, I have 500 people under me.

I'm a security guard at a cemetery.

HR: "What's your biggest weakness?"

Funny Dad: "Interviews."

HR: "And besides that?"

Funny Dad: "Follow up questions."

If an accountant's partner cannot sleep, what do they say?

"Dear, could you tell me about your work day?"z

Why was the vampire removed as CEO?

He couldn't appeal to the stakeholders.

Why was the CEO of a leading prosthetics company arrested?

It came out that he was involved in international arms dealing.

Why is money called dough?

Because we all knead it.

What's another name for long term investment?

A failed short term investment!

I saw on the news that the CEOs of T-mobile and Sprint got married last weekend.

Great wedding…

terrible reception.

After reading a bunch of "self-help" books, I've FINALLY found the secret to financial success!

I'm going to write a self-help book.

Why did the financial system collapse in ancient Egypt?

Pyramid schemes.

Guess who my financial advisor is going to be for Halloween?

Pennywise.

Why do banks have drive thru windows?

So the cars can meet their real owners.

Why are there no toilets in some banks?

Because they don't accept such deposits.

Give a man a gun and he'll rob a bank.

Give a man a bank and he'll rob the world.

What do you get when you cross a banker with a fish?

A loan shark.

I have an irrational fear of large intricate corporate buildings.

You could say I have a complex complex complex.

What's the difference between buying a lottery ticket and buying stocks?

In the first case you help finance the local community swimming pool. In the second case you help finance your stockbroker's home swimming pool.

Whenever I get a stack of resumes on my desk at work, I always pick half at random and throw them out.

Don't need unlucky people working in my department.

Boss: This is the third time you've been late for work this week. Do you know what that means?

Me: That it's only Wednesday.

My boss arrived at work in a brand new Lamborghini. I said "wow that's an amazing car."

"If you work hard, put all your hours in, and strive for excellence, I'll get another one next year."

Why do riot police like to get to work early?

To beat the crowd.

I've been fired from work for putting in too many shifts.

Keyboard manufacturing isn't as easy as you think.

Working at an unemployment office must be so tense.

Even if you get fired, you still have to come in the next day.

It must be hard for women to work in the postal service.

It's such a MAIL dominated industry.

We need somebody for this role who is responsible.

'Not a problem, sir. Every time something went wrong in my old job, my manager told me I was always responsible!'

My boss is very easygoing.

He told me not to think of him as the boss, rather, think of him as a friend who is never wrong.

Tell me, how many people work in your company?

About half!

Why did you leave your last job?

The company relocated and didn't tell me where!

My wife tells me I talk in my sleep all the time.

But I'm skeptical. Nobody at work ever mentions it.

'How well do you work with PowerPoint?'

'I think I Excel with it'

'Is that a computer joke?'

'Word.'

'Is our money all gone?'

'No, don't panic…it's just with somebody else at the moment'

How is Christmas like your job?

You do all the work and the fat guy in the suit gets all the credit!

I quit my job to start a cloning business and it's been great.

I love being my own boss.

I've just started a new business selling trampolines in Prague.

Getting a lot of orders, but the Czechs keep bouncing.

My friends and I started a business where we weigh tiny items.

It's a small scale operation.

Why did the contractor go out of business doing roofs?

Because they were always on the house.

I started a business creating religious statues…

I have yet to make a prophet.

I'm starting a business to teach short people math.

It's called, "Making The Little Things Count."

My boss is going to fire the employee with the worst posture.

I have a hunch, it might be me.

I gave up my seat to a blind person in the bus.

That is how I lost my job as a bus driver.

The Animal Lover: Paws for Laughter

One Liners!

Pig says: My name is bacon. Chris P. Bacon.

I sometimes watch birds and wonder "If I could fly, who would I crap on?"

I know everyone thinks tall people have a lot of advantages in life but in reality, we have to deal with 40% more spider webs than you do.

Squirrels always act like it's their first day of being a squirrel.

Imagine saying hello to a dog in a normal conversational voice.

As I watched the dog chasing his tail I thought "Dogs are easily amused", then I realized I was watching the dog chasing his tail.

Zebras are just horses that escaped from prison.

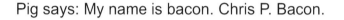

Why did the officer issue a ticket to the dog who gave birth on the side of the road?

Because she was littering.

Don't be sad when a bird craps on your head.

Be happy that dogs can't fly.

How do dog catchers get paid?

By the pound!

What kind of dog chases anything red?

A bulldog.

What kind of dog does Dracula have?

A Bloodhound.

What did the hungry Dalmatian say when he ate his dinner?

"Wow, that hit the spot!"

Why was the dog stealing shingles?

He wanted to become a woofer!

How do you know if you have a slow dog?

It chases parked cars.

Why did the Dachshund want to sit in the shade?

Because it was a hot dog.

How does a dog stop a TV show?

He presses paws.

Whenever I take my dog to the park, the ducks always try to bite him.

I guess it makes sense, since he's pure bread.

A policeman came up to me with a sniffer dog and said, "This dog tells me you're on drugs..."

I said "I'm on drugs? you're the one talking to dogs."

I'm not saying your perfume is too strong.

I'm just saying the canary was alive before you got here.

Hard to take women with false eyelashes seriously.

It's like watching two tarantulas scream for attention.

Teacher: "Name a bird with wings but can't fly."

Student: "A dead bird, sir."

I entered my Chihuahua in an 'ugliest dog' contest and I won first place!

My dog came in third.

I'll never forget my dog's last words…

"You've taken too much acid."

My wife asked me if I had seen the dog bowl.

I said "I didn't know he could!"

I was out on a first date and the lady asked me if I was more of a cat person or a dog person.

I said "I'm a vegetarian.

I spotted an albino Dalmatian the other day.

It was the least I could do.

I told my shrink I identify as a dog.

He made me get off the couch.

I think my cat might be a communist.

He won't shut up about Mao.

What's the difference between a cat and a comma?

A cat has claws at the end of paws and a comma is a pause at the end of a clause.

I don't know why everyone is saying "Cats" the movie was bad.

They played it on my flight home and there were only two walkouts.

My kids tell me that they want a cat for Christmas this year.

We normally cook a turkey for Christmas, but if they want a cat, okay.

I have a dog to provide me with unconditional love but I also have a cat to remind me that I don't deserve it.

It's all about balance.

My cat passed away but I am not sad.

She will live on forever in my online passwords.

What do you get when you crossbreed a cat with a duck?

A platypuss.

I have just found out that I'm allergic to cats.

Either that or I undercooked it.

Funny Dad was asked to feed the cat.

Funny Dad: "to what?"

Why are cats better than babies?

When you are done holding a cat you can just drop them.

Did you hear about the cat found guilty of murder?

He got nine life sentences.

My cat seems to like stormy weather...

when it rains, it purrs.

Why are cats so relaxed?

Because they live in the meow.

What's a cat's favorite way to gamble?

Scratchers.

The best beginner pet is a Hamster.

They live for 5 days and don't require any food or water.

When my pet goldfish died my parents thought it would be a great idea to replace it with a hamster...

Poor little guy drowned in seconds.

What do hamsters and cigarettes have in common?

They're both perfectly harmless until you put one in your mouth and light it on fire.

I told my son that I found his hamster in our vacuum cleaner.

With tears in his eyes he said, "Please get a new one, daddy..."

"I was thinking the same," I said, "the suction is absolutely terrible."

I drove my daughter's hamster to the vet this morning.

I'm getting pretty good at golf.

Where do hamsters go on holiday?

Hamsterdam!

What do we call a wireless mouse?

Hamster.

I went to the pet shop and asked for 12 bees.

The clerk counted out 13 bees and handed them over.

"You've given me one too many" I said.

"That one is a freebie."

A Man walks into a pet shop and asks the owner "Do you have any chameleons?"

(Looks around) No idea, man.

I entered my pet snail into a race and removed its shell thinking it would make it faster...

Unfortunately, it only made it more sluggish.

I thought that my pet alligator was going to eat me!

Turns out he was just pulling my leg.

My geometry teacher is really upset that her pet parrot died yesterday.

Polly gone.

I have two pet rats in love with each other.

They just got encaged.

My wife suggested that we should share our bed with our pets.

I finally gave in. After 10 minutes, our goldfish finally settled down.

I think my goldfish likes it when I take him out of his bowl...

He sure wags his tail a lot.

If everyone had the memory of a goldfish.

I forgot where I was going with this.....

Where does a lizard go after it drops its tail?

To the retail store.

Waves of Wit: Beach Please!

A gorgeous woman waved to me at the beach yesterday.

But there was no way I was swimming out that far to talk to her.

What does a guy with 2 right feet wear to the beach?

Flop-Flops.

I snuck onto a beach early this morning.

The coast was clear.

What type of eagle do you see at a beach?

A seagull.

The beach is very confident...

...in fact it's 100% shore.

I saw a man at the beach yelling "Help, shark! Help!"

I just laughed, I knew that shark wasn't going to help him.

So we took our new dog to the beach today.

I realize now it was not a good idea to name him Shark.

What do the Kardashians and the beach have in common?

They both contain a lot of plastic.

My latest money making idea was a rubber beach shoe for one-legged people.

It was a flop.

Watching the Olympics women's beach volleyball first round...

There's already been a wrist injury, but I should be ok by tomorrow.

What do you call something you can serve but can't eat?

A volleyball.

What was the first thing Hellen Keller noticed at the beach?

The volleyball net.

What's the best day of the week to go to the beach?

Sunday.

Did you hear about the martial artists who fought on the beach?

They faced off in sand-to-sand combat.

What do you call a beach party that gets out of hand?

Sandemonium.

Why do bananas use sunscreen?

Because they peel.

Which animal is the strongest at the beach?

The mussels.

What do you call a beach that keeps losing sand?

A shore loser.

I was so embarrassed I forgot to bring sunscreen to the beach.

Boy was my face red!

I went to a nude beach today and let me tell you, I had a lot of women's attention.

I could just feel them dressing me with their eyes.

A biologist, a physicist, and a chemist go to the beach for the first time.

The biologist is amazed at the birds, the seaweed, the fish. He goes into the water for a closer look. Pretty soon the water is over his head. He drowns.

The physicist is mesmerized by the waves. The amplitude. The periodicity. The reflections. He goes into the water for a closer look. Pretty soon the water is also over his head. He drowns.

The chemist is sitting on the beach making notes in his lab book.

He writes, "Biologists and physicists are soluble in water."

I was on the beach with my daughter.

After a while, she turned to me and said, "Dad, you look like a lobster."

"Oh no," I replied, "Am I burning?"

She said, "No. Just very ugly."

What happens when you take a nap by the ocean?

You wake up with Resting Beach Face.

What did the parasol say to the beach towel?

"I've got you covered!"

What's the most common insect found on the beach?

A beach buggy!

Where do sharks go on holiday?

Finland.

Where do scuba divers go to relax after work?

The dive bar.

I saw the shop for getting scuba diving gear was closed.

I guess it went under.

What does Sonic the hedgehog wear at the beach?

A Speedo.

Why don't sharks like fast food?

Because they can't catch it.

Life is better in sandals…

That's one opinion I will never flip-flop on.

The Techie: Bytes of Humor

One Liners!

Thanks to autocorrect, 1 in 5 children will be getting a visit from Satan this Christmas.

Are the security guys at the Samsung Store called Guardians of the Galaxy?

How many programmers does it take to change a light bulb?

None, because it is a hardware problem.

Why did the boy get fired from his keyboard factory job?

Because he was not doing enough shifts.

Why was the mobile phone wearing glasses?

Because it lost its contacts.

Why was 'beef stew' not used as a computer password?

Because it was not strong-anoff.

What kind of computer sings the best?

A Dell.

Why did the PowerPoint presentation decide to cross the road?

Because he wanted to get to the other slide.

What happens when a hard drive gets into a fight?

It asks for a back-up!

What is another name for apple juice?

iPhone chargers.

Why were the horses struggling to use the internet?

Because they were not able to find any stable connections.

The oldest computer can be traced back to Adam and Eve.

It was an apple but with extremely limited memory. Just 1 byte. And then everything crashed.

What do you call a computer mouse that swears a lot?

A cursor!

My Internet stopped working for 5 minutes.

Met my parents. They're nice people.

An Apple store near where I live got robbed. $25k worth of merchandise was stolen.

The police said that they will get both computers back.

Saw "IT" last night...

Far less "computer networking" and much more "murderous clowning" than anticipated.

I changed my password to "incorrect".

So whenever I forget what it is the computer will say "Your password is incorrect".

When I die, I want my tombstone to be a WiFi hotspot...

...that way people visit more often.

If the Internet had a boat, where would they park it?

In Google Docs!

Where does the USA keep its backups?

USB.

How can you tell when the NSA is monitoring your computer?

The power is on and you're connected to the internet.

Why do most programmers use a dark theme while coding?

Because light attracts bugs.

Why did the PowerPoint Presentation cross the road?

To get to the other slide.

Why can't you use 'Beef Stew' as a password?

Because it's not Stroganoff.

While I was driving, I saw another person driving while talking on his cell phone.

I got so mad, I threw my beer at him.

Doctor : you remind me of my cell phone

Lady: why?

Doctor: Because you're about to die

Two hunters are out in the woods when one of them collapses. He's not breathing and his eyes are glazed. The other guy whips out his cell phone and calls 911.

"I think my friend is dead!" he yells. "What can I do?"

The operator says, "Calm down. First, let's make sure he's dead."

There's silence, then a shot. The guy picks up the phone again and asks, "OK, now what?"

What do they call mobile phones in prison?

Cell phones.

Who was the first person that used technology?

Moses. He had two tablets that where connected to the cloud.

My Grandpa said, "Your generation relies too much on technology!"

I replied, "No, your generation relies too much on technology!"

Then I unplugged his life support.

My grandfather told me that teenagers have become so lazy because of technology.

"They're not the only ones," I said, looking at his mobility scooter.

I've decided to launch a brand new dating app exclusively for Palaeontologists…

I'm going to call it 'Carbon Dating.'

I'm thinking about starting a dating app for low IQ people.

I'm calling it OK Stupid.

Entered what I ate today into my new fitness app.

It just sent an ambulance to my house.

Women on dating apps give me compliments all the time.

One time this girl told me "you are unmatched."

What's the most popular dating app?

Google calendar.

You know you're texting too much when…

you try to text, but you're on a landline!

What is it called when computer programmers taunt and make fun of each other on social media?

It is called cyber boolean.

Why did the computer arrive late at work?

Because it had a hard drive.

What do you call a computer floating in the ocean?

A Dell rolling in the deep.

How does a computer get drunk?

It takes screenshots.

How did the computer get out of the house?

It used Windows.

What movies do computers love the most?

Re-boots!

Why did the computer go to the dentist?

To get its Bluetooth checked.

What do you call a superhero computer?

A screensaver.

What do computers eat for a snack?

Microchips.

How many programmers does it take to change a light bulb?

None, that's a hardware problem.

Video games are great — they let you try your craziest fantasies.

For example, on The Sims, you can have a job and a house

My life was ruined by my obsession with video games.

Fortunately, I had another two lives.

Why doesn't Mario like to use the internet?

He's afraid of the Browsers.

How do you know when a party is for a gamer?

There are tons of streamers.

Why can't PC gamers use Uber?

Too many incompatible drivers.

My girlfriend told me our relationship was over because I was spending too much time playing games.

I think it may have been my Destiny 2 breakup with her.

Why did the gamer play so many video games after his breakup?

He needed to console himself.

What do people and video games have in common?

Everyone always argues over which generation was the best.

What did the gaming reporter say about the new Minecraft updates?

"They're groundbreaking!"

And what did the movie critic say about the Minecraft movie?

"It's a blockbuster."

What did Mario say when he broke up with Princess Peach?

"It's not you; it's a me, Mario!"

I broke up with my old console.

Nothing was wrong with my Xbox, but it was time for a Switch.

Video games never made me angry or want to hurt people.

Working in customer service already did that.

My girlfriend just broke up with me for talking about video games too much...

What a stupid thing to Fallout 4.

The Guffawing Gambler: Bet You'll Laugh

What did the gambler say after his girlfriend dumped him because of his gambling addiction?

"But I know I can win her back."

People say gambling ruins lives, but it brought our family closer.

We now live in a one bedroom unit.

How can you improve Gambling addiction hotlines?

They would be so much better if every fifth caller was a winner.

How can gambling help you get back on your feet?

If you lose your car in poker.

A North Korean man frequently sneaks to the South Korean capital to gamble for bakery goods for his family.

He is the seoul breadwinner.

Why is gambling illegal in China?

Because they hate Tibet.

Did you hear about the gambler who doesn't see his wife and kids anymore?

It's all due to gambling. He won a lottery and moved to Hawai'i.

Do you know why there's no gambling in Africa?

Because there are too many cheetahs.

Why don't vampires like gambling?

They get nervous when the stakes are raised.

What did the nun wear to the casino?

Her gambling habit.

Judge asked a carpenter, "You were arrested during a drug bust in a gambling den.

What were you doing there?"

"Making a bolt for the door, your honor."

Did you hear about the paraplegic with the gambling problem?

He just couldn't walk away.

What do you call a Navy Admiral who gambles, smokes, drinks and does drugs?

A Vice Admiral.

How is Life insurance like gambling?

You: I bet you $100 I will die this year.

Insurance: We'll bet you $50,000 that you won't.

A man rushes into his house and yells to his wife, "Suzan, pack up your things. I just won ten million dollars!"

Suzan replies, "Shall I pack for warm weather or cold?"

The man responds, "I don't care. Just so long as you're out of the house by noon!"

A wife told her husband that she's had enough of his gambling, and it's time to choose between her and the horses.

He replied that it's hard enough just choosing between the horses.

Did you hear about a compulsive gambler who has finally come up with a foolproof system that will guarantee he never loses and only win?

He has started up his own online gambling company.

How do you stop a gambling addict from gambling?

Make a bet. They won't refuse.

What do you call someone that doesn't eat animal products and loves to gamble?

A Las Vegan.

What do you call a genie that loves to gamble?

A djinnerate.

How many gamblers does it take to screw in a lightbulb?

Well, all the ones we've hired so far have failed, but eventually, it'll work, I swear!

Did you hear about the gambling nurse that's doing' hard time?

She got booked for aiding and abetting.

Why was the successful gambler uncomfortable when he sat down?

He had an ace in the hole.

What do you call the toilet of a king with a gambling addiction?

Royal flush.

What do gamblers drive?

A Chevroulette.

When did Adam & Eve discover God didn't like gambling?

When he took away their pair a dice.

Do you know why the horse stalls at a racetrack are labeled A, B, D, E, and F?

Because no one would bet on a seahorse.

Why are the Irish risky gamblers?

Because they're always Dublin' down.

What's the difference between a gambler and a gardener?

One says "Read 'em and weep" the other says "Weed 'em and reap."

What's a gambler's favorite time of day?

10 to 1.

Why don't numbers gamble?

Because only alphabets.

Why gambling is like eating a bowl of pistachios?

If you get a good pistachio, you want another good one. If you get a bad one, you want a good one even more.

What kind of Gambling do depressed people always win at?

Russian Roulette.

What's the difference between a casino and a church?

You actually mean it when you pray at a casino.

What is it called when you're having second thoughts about booking a room at a Native American casino?

A reservation reservation reservation.

Why are there no casinos in France?

Because nobody likes Toulouse.

What is the worst part of selling a casino?

Everything is a gamble.

Why do fat people lose so much at casino tables?

Because whenever they are out of chips they always grab more.

Why betting your house in the casino is the best thing you can do?

The house always win.

Why was the dietician kicked out of the casino?

He was caught counting carbs.

Why wouldn't the sesame seed leave the casino?

Because he was on a roll.

A man walks into the casino and asks a security guard which machine people get the most money from.

The guard points to the ATM machine.

Why don't casinos in Las Vegas hire girls from California?

Because they, like, can't even deal.

Why is it so easy to buy drugs at a casino?

Because the casinos are full of dealers.

What's the difference between a casino and a strip club?

You actually have a chance of getting screwed at the casino.

Who's second in command at a casino restaurant?

The Sioux chef.

Did you hear about the strobe light-filled new casino for people with epilepsy?

It's called 'Seizures palace.'

Why don't tourists like the casino at Disneyland?

Because the mouse always wins.

Have you ever been to the Dad Joke Casino?

They attract a lot of Eye Rollers.

Old Folks: Time-Tested Teasers

One Liners!

I was at an ATM and this old lady asked me to help check her balance, so I pushed her over.

I saw 2 men mugging an old lady and I asked myself if I should help but decided that 3 would be overkill.

This is not what adulthood looked like in the brochure.

A diplomat is a man who always remembers a woman's birthday but never remembers her age.

I've learned that saying "Oh, this old thing?" isn't an appropriate way to introduce an elderly relative.

I don't date older women because it takes too long to listen to their life story.

The older I get, the earlier it gets late.

Being an adult is just walking around wondering what you're forgetting.

Everyone my age is older than me…

Middle age is when work is a lot less fun and fun a lot more work.

You're old enough to remember when emojis were called "hieroglyphics."

He is so old that he gets nostalgic when he sees the Neolithic cave paintings.

My teenage angst has lasted 30 years.

Middle age is when you're faced with two temptations and you choose the one that will get you home by nine o'clock.

I'm at the age where I have to make a noise when I bend over. It's the law.

Work hard and save your money and when you are old you will be able to buy the things only the young can enjoy.

I've never played the bagpipes but I have carried a screaming three-year-old toddler over my shoulder.

I don't care what you think you're good at, there's a 7-year-old kid on YouTube doing it better.

The older you get, the more you need to keep a fire extinguisher close to the cake.

Maybe adults aren't afraid of monsters under the bed anymore because we know that if we get eaten by one we won't have to go to work the next day.

I'm aging like a fine banana.

When you're wondering whether she's his daughter or his girlfriend, she's his girlfriend.

Just remember, it's better to pay full price than to admit you're a senior citizen.

I'd like to say the best moment of a woman's life is giving birth, but it's actually seeing an old nemesis and realizing she got really fat.

I'm at the age where I can't keep up with all the things I hate.

Aging gracefully is like the nice way of saying you're slowly looking worse.

Your mom's so old, her birthday candles weigh more than the cake.

Your mom's so old, her birth certificate expired.

Your mom's so old, she walked out a museum and the alarm went off.

Your mom's so old, she preordered the Bible.

They used to time me with a stopwatch...

Now they use a calendar.

How do you make an old lady say the F word?

Have another one say "Bingo!"

Transitional age is when during a hot day you don't know

what you want –

ice cream or beer.

What do call an old lady wearing camo?

Gramouflage.

My mom always used to say "40 is the new 30".

Lovely woman... banned from driving.

I like older women because they've gotten used to life's disappointments.

Which means they're ready for me.

Few women admit their age…

few men act it.

My kids are at an age now where they are beginning to understand embarrassment.

This is my time to shine.

How do you know your old?

People call at 9 p.m. and ask, "Did I wake you?"

Parenting is filled with wonder.

Like wondering why your 4 years old raced into the kitchen and quietly grabbed a handful of napkins.

I always wanted to marry an Archeologist.

The older I would get, the more interested she would become!

"Your finest Scotch, please."

"Yes, sir," the guy at Staples says as he hands me a 12 year old roll of tape.

The seven ages of man:

spills, drills, thrills, bills, ills, pills and wills.

Millennials.

Walking around like they rent the place.

Well son, in the '90s, there was no drooling emoji.

You had to show up at a girl's door and actually drool.

Should I have another baby after 35?

No, 35 children are enough.

I believe in loyalty.

When a woman reaches an age she likes, she should stick with it.

I know I'm getting old...

The other day I walked past a cemetery and two guys attacked me with shovels.

What is the main difference between men and boys?

Men's toys cost more.

Doc says to the patient, "You have the body of a twenty-year-old, but you should return it.

You're stretching it completely out of shape."

I have an 8:30 dinner reservation tonight.

That's like midnight in middle-age time.

Cults make perfect sense.

Do you know how hard it is to make friends as an adult?

What goes up and never comes down?

Your age!

Me in my 20's: "Dresses like I'm on the catwalk."

Me in my 30's: "dresses like I walk cats."

When I was young I did stupid things because I didn't know any better.

Now I know better and do stupid things because I miss being young.

I've reached the age where looking in the mirror is like

checking the news.

I know there'll be some new developments I won't like.

Son, when I was your age there was no social media.

You had to go to a bar and buy endless drinks to be ignored by multiple women.

The recommended age to have a Ouija Board is 8+ years old.

So, you need to be 21 years old to drink alcohol and 8 to summon the devil.

Wine improves with age.

I improve with wine.

One day I shall solve my problems with maturity.

Today, however, it will be alcohol.

Why did the old lady fall into the waterhole?

She couldn't see that well.

Knock, knock.

(Who's there?)
Little old lady.
(Little old lady who?)
Ah, I didn't know you could yodel.

The little old lady didn't always live in a shoe.

She once had a house, but when she couldn't pay the mortgage. The bank gave her the boot.

An old lady walks into her bank and asks the teller "Hey sonny, can you check my balance?"

So he pushed her over.

What did an old lady say after Frozone helped her across the street?

"Such an ice young man!"

The old woman who lived in a shoe wasn't the sole owner.

There were strings attached.

Did you hear about an old lady who swallowed a horse?

Her condition is stable.

What do you call an old white lady?

Gram cracker.

Why did the skeleton help the old lady cross the road?

It was no skin off his back.

Three old ladies are out for a stroll.

One of them remarks, "It's windy."

Another replies, "No way. It's Thursday."

The last one says, "Me too. Let's have a beer."

If you're driving and an old lady and a child cross the road, what do you hit first?

Hopefully the brakes.

A reporter interviewed a 103-year-old woman:

"And what is the best thing about being 103?" the reporter asked.

The woman simply replied, "No peer pressure."

What did the old woman who lived in a shoe do after she won the lottery?

She moved to Beverly Heels.

What do you call an old woman who used to model for Playboy?

A Dust Bunny.

What did the scary old woman say when she found a gold cauldron?

"I'm gonna be witch."

An old woman flew overseas for the first time.

She said that it was an uplifting experience.

How did the old woman gain hulk power?

Gramma Radiation.

What does old ladies' underwear smell like?

Depends.

What's it called when a 52 year old woman puts a stop to her online transactions?

Venmopause.

What do a werewolf and a 50-year-old woman have in common?

Nipple hair.

How do you make an old woman breathe fire?

Ignite her oxygen tank.

What do you call a woman that's old, fat, and ugly?

Your mom.

Tons of Fun with Plus-Sized Puns

One Liners!

Don't fight with me over chocolate because I am not someone to be truffled with!

You have more chins than Chinatown.

Your mom's so fat, the only good grade she got in school was an "A" in lunch.

If you weigh 200 pounds on the Earth it is only 76 pounds on Mars, and it means you are not fat but you are just on the wrong planet.

Facebook memories are a great way to see how fat you've gotten.

We shouldn't make fun of fat people because they already have enough on their plate.

A recent study has found that women who carry a little extra weight live longer than the men who mention it.

My New Year's resolution is to help all my friends gain ten pounds so I look skinnier.

Your mom's so fat, she fell down and rocked herself to sleep trying to get up!

Sometimes I go into the fitting room with jeans three sizes too big so I can feel what it's like to succeed at a diet.

Brain cells come and go but fat cells live forever.

I love my six pack so much that I protect it with layers of fat.

I don't buy fat-free milk because I don't want to contribute to cows having body issues.

You know you're fat when you step on the scale and it says "one at a time please".

You have enough fat to make another human.

Why did the lady wear a helmet every time she ate?

She was on a crash diet!

Trying to lose weight?

The center of a donut is 100% fat-free.

Your mom's so fat when she stepped on the weighing scale it said:

"I need your weight, not your phone number."

Life is like a box of chocolates;

it ends sooner for fat people.

Thanksgiving, man.

Not a good day to be my pants.

If someone calls you fat, just ignore them.

You are bigger than that!

My wife gave birth 4 times and still fits in her prom dress from high school.

I gave birth 0 times and I haven't fit in my pants since March.

Every time someone calls me fat I get so depress I cut myself...

a piece of cake.

I found there was only one way to look thin:

hang out with fat people.

Why is Christmas just like a day at the office?

You do all the work and the fat guy with the suit gets all the credit.

I wanted to lose 10 pounds this year.

Only 13 to go.

You're fat.

It's not because it runs in the family, you're fat because nobody runs in your family.

Diet Coke:

Making people feel better about ordering two Big Macs and a large fry since 1982.

Behind every fat woman there is a beautiful woman.

No seriously, you're in the way.

My weight loss goal is simple.

I just want to lie on the beach without marine biologists pouring buckets of water over me.

Doctor: "Well, it looks like you're pregnant."

Woman: "Oh my God, I'm pregnant?!"

Doctor: "No, it just looks like you are."

My wife asked me "What are the chances I will get accepted into a convent if I lose weight?"

I said "slim to nun".

My ex-girlfriend told me nothing shocks her anymore.

So I switched her digital scale from Lbs to Kg.

Fat people are lucky -

they get to eat whatever they want and not worry about getting fat.

Field of Dreams... and Chuckles

One Liners!

Being a farmer isn't for everyone, but hay, it's in my jeans.

What if soy milk is just regular milk introducing itself in Spanish?"

[Throws salad into a garden]: "Go home boy... you're free now!"

What is the difference between organic fried chicken and GMO fried chicken?

It's CRISPR.

How do you get a farm girl to like you?

A Tractor

Have you heard of the garlic diet?

You don't lose much weight, but from a distance your friends think you look thinner.

I told my wife, "Did you know Old McDonald's farm has been taken over by Artificial Intelligence?"

Her: AI?

Me: AI.
Her: Oh.

I tried to start farming crows, until I was arrested.

They charged me with attempted murder.

The internet connection at my farm was really poor, so I moved the modem to the barn.

Now I have stable wifi.

My boyfriend started a bee farm to help save the bees.

I think he's a keeper.

What's the best farm crop to vent to?

Corn.

They're all ears.

I made a movie about farm life...

...but the film quality was too grainy and the plot was very corny.

What happens when you run out of manure on a farm?

You have to make doo.

How do farmers party?

They turnip the beets.

What did the farmer say when he lost his tractor?

Where's my tractor?

A farmer was milking his cow.

At one point, he noticed a fly buzzing in the cows' ear.

Shortly after the farmer looked down at the bucket and noticed a fly swimming in the milk.

"Huh," said the farmer. "In one ear, out the udder."

A farmer had 196 cows in his field.

When he rounded them up he had 200.

What did one Dorito farmer say to the other Dorito farmer?

Cool ranch.

When did the Polish farmer get up?

At the Krakow dawn.

My farmer friend told me that horse manure is excellent for strawberries.

I said, "You may be right, but I still prefer whipped cream."

Why do goats have trouble making friends?

They always butt heads.

What did the bored goat say?

"Meh!"

What is a goat's beard called?

A goatee!

An environmentalist friend of mine told me I should buy organic because it's sustainable.

I looked at my bank account, and I really disagree.

Why did the farmer feed his pigs sugar and vinegar?

He wanted sweet and sour pork.

Why did the pig take a bath?

The farmer said "hogwash".

Why do cows have hooves instead of feet?

Because they lactose.

Why are farmers cruel?

Because they pull corn by the ears.

What are the spots on black and white cows?

Holstains.

What do you call the 200th anniversary of owning a buffalo

farm?

Bison-tennial.

Did you hear about the wooden tractor?

It had wooden wheels, a wooden engine, wooden transmission and wooden work.

How did the farmers get the highest marks in the math exams?

They were all pro-tractors.

Did you hear about the magic tractor?

It turned into a field.

What would you get after crossing a robot and a tractor?

A transfarmer.

Why did the farmer call his pig "Ink"?

Because it was always running out of the pen.

What is a sheep's favorite game?

Baa-dminton.

What did the farmer call his cow?

Pat.

What is a horse's favorite game to play?

Stable tennis.

How did the organic vegetable die?

Natural causes.

What did the corn farmer say after a good harvest?

There's polenta more where that came from.

What do you call the spirit of a dead hen haunting a farm?

A poultry-geist.

Why had the farmer buried cash in his soil?

He wanted to make his farmland rich.

Where does a farmer get his medicine from?

The farm-acist.

What happens when you get promoted as a senior director at Old MacDonald's Farm?

You are the new CIEIO.

What is similar between farms and dad jokes?

The cornier the better.

What do farmers give their wives on Valentine's Day?

Hog and kisses!

Why did the farmer only wear one boot to town?

He heard there would be a 50% chance of snow!

The Foodie: A Side of Snickers

Smoking will kill you... Bacon will kill you...

But, smoking bacon will cure it.

My parents decided the key to a successful marriage is going out to a fancy restaurant twice a week.

My dad goes out Mondays and my mom goes out Fridays.

A couple was having dinner at a fancy restaurant.

As the food was served, the husband said, "the food looks delicious, let's eat!"

The wife: Honey, you say your prayer before eating at home.

The husband: Honey, that's at home. Here the chef knows how to cook.

Just asked my wife what she's "burning up for dinner".

It turns out to be all of my personal belongings.

I ate pelican at a fancy restaurant.

The service was fantastic but the bill was enormous.

Server: So, how did you find the food sir?

Me: It was easy. You put it on a plate and kept the plate right in front of me.

I went out with my girlfriend to a fancy restaurant last night and after we'd eaten she kept insisting on paying for the meal.

I said, "Don't be stupid, we're half way down the road now. Just keep running!'

Going for a walk because I want to stay healthy.

Taking along a box of M&M's because let's be honest here.

What do you call a shish-kebab at a fancy restaurant?

A Shish-ke-Robert.

I went to a fancy restaurant last night and a man was complaining about his escargot.

The waiter just shrugged it off. "I'm sorry sir," the waiter told him. "All snails are final."

My wife asked me to take her to one of those fancy restaurants where they prepare the meal in front of you.

So I took her to Subway....

We're signing the divorce papers right now.

I got gas for $1.39 today.

Unfortunately, it was at Taco Bell.

Jesus and his disciples walk into a restaurant.

Jesus: "A table for 26, please."

Headwaiter: "But there's only... 13 of you?"

Jesus: "Yeah, we're all going to sit on the same side."

I had a Bison steak at a restaurant recently.

When I finished, I asked the waiter for the buffalo bill.

When the waitress in a New York City restaurant brought him the soup du jour, the Englishman was a bit dismayed.

"Good heavens," he said, "What is this?" "Why, it's bean soup," she replied. "I don't care what it has been," he sputtered. "What is it now?"

Why did the clock in the restaurant run slow?

It always went back four seconds!

I was at a restaurant and a waitress yelled "Does anyone know CPR?"

I said "I know the whole alphabet!" Everyone laughed, well everyone except one.

At the restaurant, my girlfriend suddenly told me, "It's over between us."

Me: "Why?"

Her: "For starters, I'm sick of your terrible jokes."

Me: "Ok. And for the main course?"

A Mexican guy and his pet otter go to a restaurant, sit down at a table, and place their order.

They are in for an early dinner and are the only customers. The chef looks down at the order slip and says incredulously: "Who comes to a restaurant and orders a whole raw fish?"

His sous chef scans the restaurant, sees his only two customers, and replies: "It's either Juan or the otter."

Did you hear about the Mexican restaurant that only serves Indian food?

Turns out the chef is a naan-conformist!

A restaurant owner offered me a free calamari appetizer if I gave him a good review on Yelp.

It was squid pro quo.

A waiter walks up to a table full of Jewish women dining:

"Ladies, is anything ok?"

To teach kids about democracy, I let them vote on dinner.

They just picked pizza.

I'm about to make tacos because they don't live in a swing state.

If Queen Elizabeth accidentally farts during dinner, the other guests are supposed to pretend like nothing happened.

Noble gasses should have no reaction.

If you could have dinner with any historical figure, who would you choose?

"Gandhi."

Why him?

"More food for me."

Why did Han Solo cry during his steak dinner?

Because it was Chewie.

My next door neighbor just knocked on my door with her dinner in her hands.

With Facebook and Instagram down she wanted me to see what she was having.

What do nuclear radiation specialists have for dinner?

Fission chips!

What does an introverted vegan want for dinner?

Peas and quiet.

My wife asked me, "Why don't you treat me like you did when we were first dating!?"

So I took her to dinner and a movie...

Then dropped her off at her parents' house.

We were eating dinner tonight, when my daughter said to me, "I see your glass is empty. Would you like another one?"

I said, "Why would I want two empty glasses?"

What do you call two foodies that go out to dinner together?

Taste buds!

My wife asked if she could have a little peace and quiet while she cooked dinner.

So I took the battery out of the smoke detector.

I was having dinner with Garry Kasporov and there was a check tablecloth.

It took him two hours to pass me the salt.

I was going to cook alligator for dinner.

But then I realized I only have a croc pot.

"Dad, are bugs good to eat?" asked the boy. "Let's not talk about such things at the dinner table, son," his father replied.

After dinner the father inquired, "Now, son, what did you want to ask me?"

"Oh, nothing," the boy said. "There was a bug in your soup, but now it's gone."

What did Nixon say when asked to help with the presidential dinner?

"I am not a cook!"

A cannibal showed up late to a dinner.

He ended up getting the cold shoulder.

If I bring you breakfast in bed, just say, "Thanks."

Not "Who are you?" and "How did you get in my apartment?"

Two things you can't eat for breakfast.

Lunch and dinner.

My wife warned me to stop making breakfast puns…

She said I'd be toast. I replied, our son keeps egging me on, he's such a ham.

What's the worst kind of jam for breakfast?

Traffic jam.

My waitress at breakfast this morning was really unsettling.

She gave me the crêpes.

My 12 year old son tried coffee for the first time today.

"It tastes like dirt!"

I told him it was just ground this morning.

Instead of water, I put redbull in the the back of my coffee maker this morning

I was halfway to work before I realized I forgot my car.

A newlywed couple lay in bed one morning and the husband says: "How about you go brew us some coffee?"

Wife: "That's your job."

Husband: "Says who?"

Wife : "The bible, it's on just about every page."

Husband: "The bible doesn't say anything about brewing coffee."

Wife (Holding her Bible flipping pages): "See every page Hebrews, Hebrews, hebrews."

Retired Life: Knot Working Anymore

One Liners!

Retirement kills more people than hard work ever did.

The question isn't at what age I want to retire, it's at what income.

The best time to start thinking about your retirement is before the boss does.

Retirement is the time in your life when time is no longer money.

The reason grandchildren and grandparents get along so well is because they have a common "enemy".

A retired husband is often a wife's full-time job.

Somewhere an elderly lady reads a book on how to use the internet, while a young boy googles "how to read a book".

Money isn't everything but it sure keeps you in touch with your children.

Work hard and save your money and when you are old you will be able to buy the things only the young can enjoy.

To be old and wise, you must first be young and stupid.

Don't mess with old people, life imprisonment is not that much of a deterrent anymore.

Retirement is what you do between doctor appointments.

The company gave me an aptitude test and I found out the work I was best suited for was retirement.

Retirement: the pay sucks, but the hours are really good!

Retirement is the part of life when the most difficult thing to do is nothing.

When a professional golfer retires what exactly does he do?

I can't wait to retire so I can get up at 6 o'clock in the morning and go drive around really slow and make everybody late for work.

Congratulations on quitting your job without being escorted out of the building!

If Christ were alive today, he'd have a huge retirement account because Jesus saves.

When I told the doctor about my loss of memory, he made me pay in advance.

Grandma's been staring through the window ever since it started to snow.

If it gets any worse I'll have to let her in.

My grandfather tried to warn them about the Titanic.

He screamed and shouted about the iceberg and how the ship was going to sink, but all they did was throw him out of the theater.

Another World's Oldest Man has died.

This is beginning to look suspicious.

Retirement is wonderful.

It's doing nothing without worrying about getting caught at it.

Why do retirees smile all the time?

Because they can't hear a word you're saying!

When is a retiree's bedtime?

Three hours after he falls asleep on the couch.

Age is an issue of mind over matter.

If you don't mind, it doesn't matter.

How many retirees to change a light bulb?

Only one, but it might take all day.

I was thinking about how people seem to read the Bible a whole lot more as they get older.

Then it dawned on me ... they were cramming for their finals.

How can you tell that you're getting old?

You go to an antique auction and three people bid on you!

Back in my day, we didn't watch TV while we ate dinner.

We actually talked to each other. It was awful.

My wife and I have started aggressively planning for our retirement…

And by that I mean we're playing the lottery 3-5 times per week.

Who are the hardest people to convince to retire?

Children at bedtime.

Why did the butcher retire?

He was cut off in his prime!

How do you know you're old enough to retire?

Instead of lying about your age you start bragging about it!

I hear retirement is lonely. I hope you don't get lonely.

If you do, don't call me. I'll be at work.

How do you know someone's retired?

They ask you, "Hey, what day is it?"

When do mushrooms retire?

When they get too mold.

What do gardeners do in retirement?

Not mulch.

I love doing stand up comedy at the retirement homes.

And I know I'm really good because they laugh at the same jokes every week.

After seeing a co-worker win the Powerball, my retirement plan has changed.

It's back to $20 million.

My work offered to fund my retirement account in soup exclusively...

...I'm the first person to have a Broth IRA.

I'm coming out of retirement to build tiny houses.

I just need a little structure.

I'm going to be a DJ at a retirement home this weekend.

With an average age of 81 years old, will the song "Last Christmas" be inappropriate?

What do retirement homes smell like?

Depends.

Did you hear about the new Bruce Willis movie?

Bruce Willis has to go undercover in a retirement home for nuns to stop a terrorist plot.

It's called "Old Habits Die Hard".

Where do cannibals go to buy their veggies?

A retirement home.

I would never put my parents in a nursing home.

I can't afford it.

How can you tell it's a Millennial nursing home?

All the residents have atrophy.

Grandad went into a nursing home, so I rang them to see how he was.

Nurse said, "He's like a fish out of water."

I said, "So he's finding it hard to adjust?"

She said, "No, he's dead!"

What did the old man say to the prettiest nurse at the nursing home?

"Help! I've fallen for you and I can't get it up!"
I used to work at a nursing home full of handicapped people.

But I quit, because I could not stand them.

What do you tell your grandmother when she doesn't want to go to a nursing home?

"It won't be for long."

Bonus Jokes! Just for Father's Day!

If a mother is laughing at the fathers jokes, it means they have guests.

Fathers Day is just like Mothers Day, only you don't spend as much.

I would give my dad what he really wants on Father's Day, but I can't afford to move out yet.

Last Father's Day my son gave me something I always wanted: the keys to my car.

Becoming a father is easy enough, but being one can be very rough.

Being a great father is like shaving. No matter how good you shaved today, you have to do it again tomorrow.

Remember: What dad really wants is a nap. Really.

Why are Fathers like parking spaces? The good ones are already taken!

What do toys and boobs have in common? Both are made for children but it's the fathers who play with them most.

And there you have it, dear reader, the culmination of a year's worth of laughter, groans, and those priceless moments where humor bonds families and friends. As you reach the end of "Dad Jokes 2024," we want to extend our sincerest thanks for being a part of this journey.

Like a hearty chuckle shared at the dinner table or a well-timed quip during a road trip, your presence as a reader has added an extra layer of joy to this book. You've embarked on a whimsical adventure through the world of dad humor, and we hope it has brought a smile to your face, an eye-roll or two, and perhaps even a moment of reflection on the beauty of shared laughter.

If you found yourself grinning, groaning, or even shaking your head in disbelief at the puns and one-liners contained within these pages, <u>we kindly ask you to consider sharing your thoughts on Amazon</u>. Your reviews help spread the infectious joy of dad jokes to others who may be in dire need of a good laugh.

Remember, the power of laughter is a wonderful thing, and in these pages, you've unlocked its potential to brighten your day and those around you. May these jokes serve as your trusty companions, ready to whisk away any clouds of seriousness that may threaten to loom overhead.

In parting, we offer you our warmest wishes for many more moments of unbridled laughter, playful eye-rolls, and the sweet camaraderie that can only be found in the world of dad jokes.

With chuckles and gratitude,
Alex

Made in the USA
Columbia, SC
19 December 2023

29065806R00059